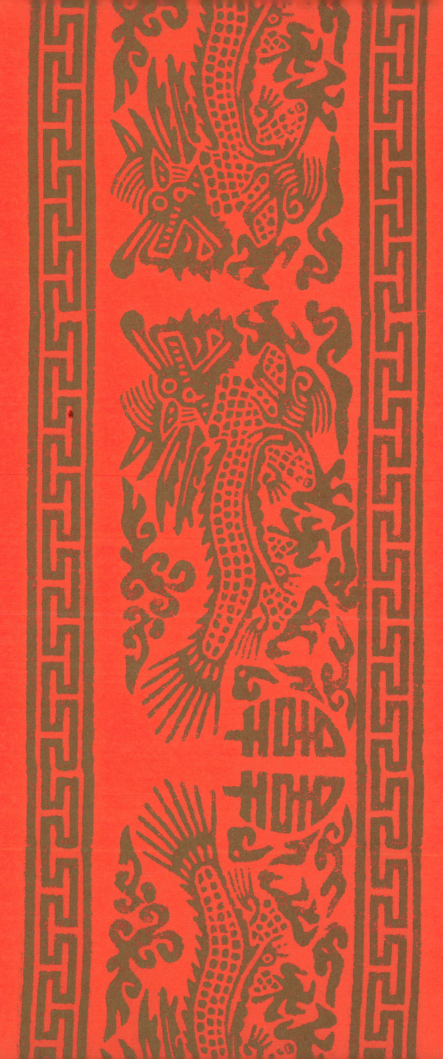

Quilting in the Morning Calm

Floral Delights from Ancient Korea

The Carriage Trade Press
P.O. Box 51491 Eugene, OR 97405
http://www.carriagetradepress.com

Quilting in the Morning Calm
Floral Delights from Ancient Korea
by Shirley MacGregor & Sheila Steers

ISBN 0-9671433-3-0

Editing
Douglas MacGregor
Margaret Tusko

Translation & Communication
Ok Sun Chang
Chin Yong Kim

Cover Design & Photography
Shirley Macgregor

Library of Congress Control Number
2002091521

Published by The Carriage Trade Press
P. O. Box 51491, Eugene, Oregon 97405
http://www.carriagetradepress.com
email: info@carriagetradepress.com

Copyright © 2002 by The Carriage Trade Press. All right reserved. No part of this book may be reproduced in any form, unless otherwise stated. All text, diagrams, patterns and photographs found herein are specifically intended for the use of the purchaser. None of the text and / or images in this book may be reproduced by any electronic, mechanical, or other means, including information storage or retrieval systems, for commercial use. Questions regarding the use of these materials should be directed to The Carriage Trade Press. Copyrights on all quilts shown in this book are retained by the individual artists.

Printed in the Republic of Korea
by
Ulchi Gracom Ltd.
email: gunngook@hitel.net

Dedications

To Richard, my husband and best friend, for all of your encouragement and support.

— Sheila

and,

To Esther LaPearl MacGregor & Grace LaPearl, two women cut from the same cloth as Sim Saim-dang.

and,

To Doug for all the help, love and understanding.

— Shirley

Acknowledgments

• To all the quilt artists who have so generously given there time, energy, and talent to make this book possible. May your paths be strewn with beautiful fabric.

• To the Republic of Korea and the many fine people with whom we have come in contact. May the bond of friendship between our two countries become even stronger in years to come.

• Yoon, Ja Yoon and staff of the Korean National Museum

• Ojuk'on Museum Kangnung City

Special Thanks

To Elaine La Blanc, who passed on a love of sewing and fabrics to a daughter who now makes very few clothes, but lots of quilts.

— Sheila

Jung Sun Kim for providing needed resources

Sound Advice and Moral Support

Nicki Frasier

And to anyone we have left out, our most profound apology.

Index

Acknowledgements

Table of Contents

I. Introductory Notes
    A Word About Korea 4
    Sim Saimdang 8

II. Purpose and Scope 6

Chapter 1.   A Quilter's Tale - Glenda Beasley 11

Chapter 2.   Two Mice and Watermelon 15

Chapter 3.   Two Plants 21

Chapter 4.   Frog 26

Chapter 5.   Two Pumpkins 35

Chapter 6.   Loofa 43

Chapter 7.   Two Beetles 51

Chapter 8.   Eggplant 59

III. Instructions 64

IV. Patterns 68

V. Suggested Reading 91

VI. References

A Word About Korea

Situated precariously between China and Japan, Korea has faced attack and domination by foreign powers for centuries. The most recent conflict, from 1950 to 1953, left the entire peninsula in ruin, bitterly divided, and desperately poor. Koreans are a very resourceful people, though, and they have risen quickly from the devastation of war to make South Korea one of the leading industrial nations of the world—and all in less than 50 years! It is said that Mikhail Gorbachev, when

asked what prompted him to turn the Soviet Union toward a market economy, said it was Korea's example that changed his thinking.

Since the war, the Republic of Korea has experienced truly astounding growth in all aspects of its society, especially within the past 20 years. With increasing prosperity, and relations with North Korea somewhat more relaxed (keeping in mind that a state of war still exists between the two countries), the Korean people are at last able to turn their attention to their ancient and unique cultural heritage. What they have accomplished in that regard is quite remarkable, too, considering that the country's art and culture were virtually obliterated by the Japanese occupation that lasted from the late 1890s until the end of World War II. In recent years, however, museums and cultural centers have sprung up, and Korean artists in ever-increasing numbers are sharing their gifts with the world.

Characterized as "the Irish of Asia," the Korean people are more apt to show their emotions than others in the region, which is probably why Westerners tend to feel more comfortable among them. Their lively spirit can be seen in day-to-day activities and in their colorful traditional dress. And it can be tasted in the spicy food that makes dining in Korea such a memorable event.

Seoul, South Korea's capital, sitting comfortably astride the Han River, is a sprawling metropolis of more than thirteen million people. The city has made impressive strides in recent years, helped in part by hosting the 1988 Olympic Games, and more recently by the 2002 World Cup soccer tournaments, which were hosted jointly with Japan. Public transportation in the capital is very good, with a first-rate subway system and reasonably priced buses and taxis.

Seoul is also a shopper's paradise, with a dizzying variety of quality merchandise on sale in a wide range of outlets, from old-world street markets to posh departments stores. Prices rival any in Asia, and are often negotiable.

For the quilter, Seoul approaches heaven on earth. In Dongdaemun, or the "east gate" area, near the city's center, is located what has to be one of the world's biggest fabric markets. Here, several factory-size buildings are filled with bolts of fabric of every description, along with bins full of buttons and other accessories in quantities that boggle the mind. This impressive wholesale market feeds Korea's massive clothing industry, but a good many of the vendors, whose small concessions dot the corridors of the buildings like cells in a beehive, are more than willing to dispense a yard or two of fabric to an eager quilter.

If you are planning a trip to Asia, be sure to include a visit to the The Republic of Korea, Land of Morning Calm. The people are helpful and friendly, the streets are safe day or night, prices are low and the quality of the merchandise first rate. Above all, you will find a very unique and colorful Asian culture that rivals any in the region.

Purpose

Something old, something new, something borrowed from another culture, and another time. What an exciting project, to take paintings that are almost five centuries old, from an ancient Asian culture, and give them new life in a very different and very dynamic artistic medium. That was the motivation for *Quilting in the Morning Calm*. And as you can see by the quilts presented here, the dream has become a stunning reality.

We have tried in several ways to provide inspiration for others to participate in this small renaissance. First, the quilters chosen for the project represent a wide range of skill levels. Some are virtual newcomers, with just a few years at the hoop. Others come with credentials that make some of us feel pretty humble. All, however, are quilters in the true sense of the word.

There are five different nationalities represented in the book, with quilters from Britain, New Zealand, Canada, Korea, and various parts of the United States. Others of us have been kicking around the world for so long that we feel at home just about anywhere. We feel that such cultural diversity adds a richness to the interpretation to the paintings.

You may have noticed that the book is filled with color. We did this to show the quilts as they should be shown, and to place them in a context that is authentic and inspiring. And what is more inspiring to a quilter than color?

We have included brief biographical notes on each of the quilters involved in the project, as well as some of their comments concerning their efforts, and on quilting in general. We hope that these notes will allow you to become a little better acquainted with the people who gave the time, energy and talent needed to bring the pages of this book to life.

The floral patterns included in the book are as true to the original paintings as we could make them. We considered placing them on a CD, but finally concluded that full-size fold-outs, with supplemental page-size patterns, are still more "user friendly."

The border patterns are truly authentic Korean designs. They can be found on ancient artifacts and buildings, and also in the bright fabrics of Korean traditional dress.

Quilting in Korea is still in its infancy, but growing very rapidly. In the past, Korean quilters have focused their attention almost entirely on American and Japanese styles. But now many are discovering worthy themes in their own rich cultural heritage. We wholeheartedly support this transition, and hope that we have helped it along with the publication of this book.

Scope

We didn't want this to be "just another quilt book," and for better or for worse, we feel we've succeeded in that regard. The focus of course is appliqué, so we have included some rather general instructions which will help you along if you have a fair idea what you are doing. If you don't, then pick up a few of the many fine books listed in the *References* section. The authors of these books have done a splendid job of explaining a variety of different approaches to appliqué, and we believe that you will find their instructions easy to follow and enjoyable to read.

Finally, there is a fairly comprehensive list of materials which we believe will help to make appliqué a civilized pursuit. Try them and you will see that necessity (or perhaps frustration) was the mother many of these inventions.

We invite you to join us on our adventure into early Korean art, and hope that *Quilting in the Morning Calm* inspires you to look deeper into this fascinating culture.

Shirley and Sheila

Sim Saimdang 1504 -1551
Photo courtesy of Ojuk'on Museum Kangnung City

Sim Saimdang

Quilting in the Morning Calm focuses on the work of Sim Saimdang,[1] a remarkable woman who has earned a very significant place in Korea's history and culture.

She was remarkable not only because she was an accomplished artist and poet in an age where such pursuits were forbidden to women of her class, but also because for almost 500 years she has been revered by Koreans as the model mother and wife.

Born into a privileged family in Kangwon Province in October 1504, Sim Saimdang was schooled in the Chinese classics. She is said to have shown exceptional artistic talent at a very early age, and she began to copy the paintings of renowned fifteenth-century Korean painter Ahn Kyon with remarkable accuracy.

Married at nineteen, Saimdang produced seven children. Most notable among them was Yi I, or Yulgok (1536–84),[2] who achieved fame as one of Korea's most significant Neo-Confucian philosophers and statesmen. It was she who schooled the young prodigy in the classical literature of China, which led to his remarkable rise into the hierarchy of the Chosun government. And it was her son's celebrity that brought the virtues and accomplishments of Sim Saimdang to the knowledge of the Korean people.

To understand the conditions under which Sim Saimdang lived, it is necessary to know a bit about the social norms that existed during the Chosun Dynasty (1392–1910), and of the Neo-Confucian philosophy that permeated the Korean peninsula at that time.

Through the ages, Korean culture has been heavily influenced by China, and it was through the Chinese that the teachings of *K'ung Fu-Tzu*, or Confucius (551–479 B.C.), entered Korean society. Confucius lived in a chaotic era of Chinese history, and his ethical concepts brought reason and stability where little had existed before. He was an early advocate of family unity, and was also a strong proponent of such revolutionary ideas as justice, ethical use of power, education on the basis of merit instead of privilege, and loyalty. Unfortunately, this sense of justice did not apply to women, whom he placed in a strictly subordinate position to men. The following is an example of such thinking:

> Man is the representative of Heaven and is supreme over all things. Woman yields obedience to the institutions of man and helps him to carry out his principles. On this account she can determine no thing of herself and is subject to the rule of the Three Obediences. When young, she must obey her father and elder brother; when married, she must obey her husband; when her husband is dead, she must obey her son. She may not think of marrying a second time.[3]

Although Confucian thinking had been a significant influence on the Korean Peninsula for centuries, it experienced a strong resurgence during the Chosun Dynasty, when the leadership pushed Buddhism aside. A very strict interpretation of Confucian principles was combined with existing beliefs to form Korean Neo-Confucianism, which focused very keenly on every aspect of human interaction. Filial piety—devotion to family, with a male figure at its head—became the cornerstone of Korean society, and the concept still wields a great deal of influence today.

Women of prominent families during the Chosun period were most certainly privileged, as their creature comforts were met and they were protected from the arbitrary treatment suffered by many in the lower classes. These comforts came at a very high price, however, as women were severely restricted in a great many ways. Basically, they could do nothing that might in any way damage the reputation of the head of the household, or that of the head of state to whose court the family was attached. Thus they were obliged to obey a strict code of behavior specified by the government. Ladies of such families were kept indoors most of the time, and they were forbidden from participating in activities that were reserved for the *kisaeng*—women similar to the *geisha* of Japan—who were highly trained in music, dance, poetry and painting, for the purpose of entertaining men.

In spite of these severe restrictions, Sim Saimdang managed to exercise her ample talents through painting, embroidery, calligraphy, and poetry, and she produced some of the finest work of her time.

Hollyhoch and Frog   Photo courtesy of the Korean National Museum

1.   Saimdang is a pen name that this illustrious lady used during her lifetime. *Sim* is also written as *Sin* and *Shin*.
2.   Yulgok was a pen name. His true name was *Yi I*, sometimes written *Yi Yi*.
3.   *The Wisdom of Confucius*, p. 63, The Peter Pauper Press, Mount Vernon, NY, 1963.

How Did My Garden Grow?

by Glenda Beasley

When the invitation to participate in this project came, it was addressed to those quilters who love to appliqué. Well, I did not qualify on those grounds, as appliqué is hardly my favorite quilting technique. However, I love to quilt, and I love to have my quilts published, so I begged to be included in this project. I questioned my sanity several times over the following months, but managed to overcome most obstacles, with a lot of help and encouragement from my friends.

My first order of business was to shop, which is one of my favorite things about making any quilt. In fact, I enjoy it so much, I have about 3,000 pounds of fabric in my stash already. But that didn't stop me from buying more fabric for this quilt. I live in Doha, Qatar, in the Middle East, where the fabric market leaves a lot to be desired. Fortunately, I was headed back to America, otherwise known as "Land of Many Quilt Shops," for a vacation. After an Internet search to determine what a loofah plant looks like, and what colors I should be looking for, it was time to do some damage to the credit card. So, I headed off for the USA, where my family and friends would be my accomplices for this mission.

I hit every fabric store and quilt shop I could find in every area I visited on my five-week trip to America. I started out easy, concentrating on the chain stores, and managed to visit Wal-Mart, Hancock's, JoAnn's, Hobby Lobby, and several locally owned fabric outlets. I hit every quilt shop I could find, and "let my fingers do the walking" to be sure I found them all! I was like a kid in a candy store. I bought thread for piecing, appliqué, embroidery and quilting. I stocked up on needles for appliqué, quilting, embroidery and sewing machines. I purchased new scissors, rulers, safety pins, bias tube makers and a book on appliqué. And most of all, I bought fabric—fabric for backgrounds, backings, borders, leaves, vines and flowers. I bought about four times more than I needed, but more is better, right?

Not satisfied with the shopping options in southern Illinois, my mom and I set out for new adventures in Kentucky, home of Hancock's of Paducah. There we met up with a friend from my two-year stay in Korea. We were shopping buddies back then, so it was only natural that we meet up for some serious shopping again. We talked and shopped as fast as we could, trying to catch up on our lives, and collect as much fabric as possible in two hours. We said our good byes, and then I was off to deal with our broken rental car. The rental company was wise to yield on this one, and cough up a new car, instead of fixing the old one. I had no time to spare—I was a quilter on a mission in Quilt City, USA!

The rental car unpleasantness settled, it was on to the American Quilt Society Museum for some inspiration. I could not have planned my visit any better, for as I walked in, what to my wondering eyes should appear?—a whole room full of Korean quilts! I had stumbled upon an exhibit fielded by Barbara Eikmeier, featuring the work of a number of very talented Korean quilt artists. I soaked up the atmosphere, and studied every caption on every photo, recognizing people and places that I had left only eighteen months before. I carefully studied all the quilts for technique, hoping that my Korean quilt would be worthy of such an exhibition.

The next phase of my adventure brought more shopping, and some invaluable help from some very special friends in northern Virginia. I was delighted to find that my hostess, Susie Johnson, had graciously planned a full itinerary of quilty activities for me. First, we headed up to Pennsylvania Amish country, where we shopped at Sauder's in Denver, and Zook's in Intercourse. The next day at a tea party/show-and-tell, I was able to visit with many old friends, make some new ones, and see some very beautiful quilts. Of course, all *I* had to show was a line drawing and a pile of fabrics, but all of my friends were very supportive and encouraging. I received lots of good suggestions and advice for my new quilt that day.

At one point it felt like we were playing on some new TV game show while discussing my quilt. Pat said she could make that quilt in one month using needle-turn appliqué. Susie said she could do it with a glue stick in one week. And Anne said she could do it in one day using freezer paper with the shiny side on the back. Hmmm, OK. Anne was clearly the winner, and I decided I would use her technique.

The next day there was an emergency run to the quilt and fabric shops to buy a little iron so I could actually start on the quilt. Then, with free rein in Susie's studio, I attempted to prepare my pieces for freezer paper appliqué. Oh my, what a humbling experience. My pieces were lumpy and bumpy, nothing like the smooth curves and sharp points I would need for this project. Susie returned from work to give me a demonstration in glue stick technique, and a new method for making vines with narrow strips of fabric cut on the bias. She also helped me simplify some of the more intricate leaf designs.

The next day my friends Pat Alfredson and Anne Oliver took me out for a delicious southern lunch before we met with my old quilting group from a year in the D.C. area. I brought along my pitiful examples of freezer paper preparation for some assistance from an expert (Anne won Best of Show at AQS in Paducah with her quilt, *Mamma's Garden*, and her *Painted Metal Ceiling* was voted one of The Twentieth Century's Best American Quilts). I had my freezer paper pattern pieces for the six large leaves, my fabric and the little iron with me. Anne considered my problem for a few minutes, then she gathered up the pieces and said she would get back with me. About two hours later she delivered the perfectly prepared pieces, all ready to be sewn to the background.

Too soon, I was back in Qatar, facing a very short deadline to finish the quilt. I jumped right in, and with a lot of trial and error, actually managed to make the quilt. It wasn't always smooth sailing, and there was an awful lot of "reinventing the wheel" involved. I used many different appliqué techniques, and the dimensional pieces proved to be the most troublesome. I found novelty fabrics to use for the grasshopper and butterflies, and I tried several different methods for the flowers before I was satisfied. Then, with the clock ticking ever louder, and me with no embroidery skills, it was time to call on the services of another good friend, Andy Bailey. She came over for two days and embroidered the details that brought my quilt to life. In the meantime, I was piecing the borders as quickly as possible. Once the entire top was embellished and finished, it was time for the quilting. I hand-quilted around all the appliqué pieces, then resorted to machine-quilting the border and background. I was just finishing up the binding when Andy stopped by to take digital photos for me. She found me in despair, unable to find a shipping company that could deliver the quilt on time. She also caught me red-handed, eating chocolate chips and drinking Diet Coke for breakfast. After a pep talk and a photo session, I found a company that promised delivery by the deadline. I quickly added a label, gently packed it, and sent my little *Loofah Garden* on its way to Seoul. Little did I know that this "quick shipping" ploy would turn into a nightmare.

Just as I was starting to breathe a little more easily, I received word from Shirley that my quilt was hung up at customs. The barbarian tasked with inspecting goods entering Korea at the shipping company had decided that this was a commercial item and added a $100 customs fee to an already outrageous shipping charge. To add insult to injury, the wannabe customs agent had pulled my precious quilt from its secure shipping tube, then proceeded to stuff it back in. It arrived in a crumpled mass at Shirley's doorstep—and three days late at that! Rage bubbled up on both sides of the ocean, and unbridled wrath descended upon the shoulders of those at the shipping company from as many sources as we could muster. A *real* Korean customs agent supported our claim, and the company agreed to withdraw the duty fee, and refund the shipping charge. Meanwhile, Shirley had steamed out the wrinkles in time for the photo shoot. All's well that ends well, I guess.

As I reflect on the making of this quilt, I realize that I learned, and re-learned, many important lessons. I truly love to quilt, and although I still prefer to piece, I don't hate or even *dislike* appliqué. I found myself planning more projects to use all the silk thread left over from this project. I decided that it is easier to quilt in America, where there are fabric stores or quilt shops in almost every town. And it is much easier to obtain quilting supplies when using your native tongue. I realized that it is much easier for me to quilt with the encouragement and help of good friends. Without the assistance and encouragement I received along the way, I might still be sitting with a pile of fabric and a line drawing. At the very least, there would have been a much less successful quilt.

Quilting gives me time to reflect on various aspects of my life. I thought of my dad, who always raised a wonderful garden. I'm sure he would have planted some loofahs for me to compare to my finished quilt, if he were alive. I thought about my mom, who taught me to sew at an early age. She sewed out of necessity, as well as for relaxation. I got my love of sewing from her. Various quilting teachers and friends helped me learn new techniques, or pushed me to try new things.

As I struggled to conquer the challenges in this quilt, I even considered forcing myself to learn techniques I never intended to use, and buy books I'd never considered before, just so I could be prepared for future challenges. I did talk myself out of that idea, though, as life is too short to spend doing things I don't enjoy. A little challenge is fine, but I decided I could continue to swap favors with friends for services I can't perform for myself. And some day soon I'll be in America again, where there are quilt guilds with libraries.

I put a lot of thought into the name of my quilt. I sewed at the dining room table, watching the gardener who came every afternoon to tend to the flowers in my yard. Occasionally I would show him how the quilt was coming along. I told him I was growing a loofah garden in fabric, and the name seemed just right.

I think my efforts on *Loofah Garden* were successful, as it gave me enjoyment while I was working on it, and when it was finished I was satisfied. It gave me time to reflect on the two years I spent in Korea, and the many wonderful people I met there. The border is a wonderful frame and gives the effect of looking at a garden scene through a window.

Chapter 2
Two Mice and Watermelon

34.5" x 29.5"
Karen Glover   Seoul, South Korea

"My mother used to have nightmares when she saw me heading to her sewing machine to make Barbie clothes when I was six. I did survive without sewing my fingers together. After taking a quilting course in 1985, I was captivated. I work mostly with cotton prints, adding texture to my quilts with both hand and machine embroidery. Primarily I work with the sewing machine but have been known to do hand appliqué. I now live in Seoul, South Korea, after a move from Halifax, Nova Scotia, in 2001.

"In making my quilt I started by pulling fabrics for the watermelon and cutting a piece of fusible web for the basic shape. I did not use the fusible web under the pink fleshy part of the watermelon, as that is a sheer fabric and the fused texture would show.

"I tried to take advantage of shading and preexisting designs in printed fabrics and tested several different fabrics before settling on what to use for various elements in the design."

In layering several fabrics that have fusible web attached, the appliqué can become stiff and difficult to sew. To avoid this Karen used a small amount of water-soluble glue to hold the fabrics while stitching. She found flat oval shapes made from abalone shells at the button market in Seoul, drilled holes in them, and stitched them to the quilt for the watermelon seeds.

Once satisfied with the placement of the appliqué elements, Karen started to machine-appliqué. "I discovered that the zigzag stitch did not work on my sewing machine. A lot of handwork followed with both embroidery floss and pearl cotton thread to finish the edges of the watermelon and butterflies." Karen used silk ribbon to embroider lazy daisy stitches as delicate leaf and flower detail, and gave the leaves a raw-edge finish.

The inside of the larger watermelon has a textured center to give it a more realistic look. The geometric design at the top of the quilt is a typical feature seen on garden walls and buildings in Korea. To create the border design, Karen glued a suede ribbon into place and then topstitched it. Scallops at the top of the quilt represent roof tiles.

Watermelon and Mice 36.25" x 40.5"
Betty Buckley   Fayetteville, Arkansas

"At age sixty-seven, I have been married fifty years and have five children and seven grandchildren. I have been sewing since I was twelve years old. When my husband was in the Army I taught sewing classes to military wives. I spent the first thirty-three years of married life sewing, doing knitting and crochet, needlepoint and cross-stitching. During those times I could almost always find a military wife who also enjoyed these types of needlework. THEN I found quilting.

"In 1985 I took my first class and was IMMEDIATELY involved. I have attended every AQS quilt show and workshop since their beginning 17 years ago. The classes I have taken gave me the confidence to teach and try new designs on my own. I love to try new fabrics. I guess my favorite technique is reverse appliqué. I love handwork of all kinds because it is soothing and keeps the stress down.

"The design that was given to me was Sim Saimdang's 'Mice and Watermelons.' I was given the freedom to do what I wanted in making the quilt. I chose cotton fabrics, two pieces of silk brocade that I received from Shirley, and Ultrasuede. The watermelons and stems were hand-appliquéd. The watermelons were lightly stuffed before appliquéing them to the background. The small stems on the vines were embroidered by hand using three shades of green. The mice and seeds are made with Ultrasuede. Silk organza was machine-embroidered between two layers of Solvy to create the three-dimensional effect of the attached butterflies. The flowers were made using some of the Korean fabric sent to us by Shirley. I machine-appliquéd all the leaves and machine-quilted the quilt.

"Problems? When I first received my design, I thought 'silk.' After trying several pieces, this thought changed to cotton. I had three choices of background but the one I finally used was the most dramatic. I had the watermelons and all the leaves cut out to use like 'paste-ups' to help decide placement. I tried felt and the Ultrasuede for the mice and the suede fabric won.

"After I had taken a class from Kumiko Sudo and learned her way to finish a quilt, I found this method suited me best, especially since I had used red fabric to brighten up the quilt."

Betty also added some detail to the watermelons with paint. Betty lives with her family in Fayetteville, Arkansas, and has taught quilting classes at quilt shops and quilt guilds in the area.

Chapter 3
Two Plants

Hands Behind My Back   33" x 41.5"
Ruth Bass   Springfield, Oregon

"My love of quilting began at the tender age of five. My grandmother used to show me quilt tops she and my great-grandmother had made. She told me the names of the patterns, but I was more interested in the multitude of colors. Colors continued to excite me, and over the years I took many art classes and read about art. After time spent raising a family, I became a co-owner of a quilt shop in 1995. The excitement of working with such wonderful fabric colors led me to finding my artist's way again. I took a quilt class and produced a work I called *Breaking Free*. I have continued to create fabric art.

"Upon seeing the design, I was surprised to find a delicate rendering of plants and insects I didn't recognize. I was assigned to do a traditional interpretation of the design. My goal was to create a wall hanging resembling a pen-and-ink drawing on aged rice paper, colored with watercolor paints."

Ruth's large plant was identified as a garden balsam and she chose to reproduce it in fuchsia and burgundy batiks. Batiks are excellent to use with fusible appliqué, as they do not fray easily. Ruth used colors found in the bull thistle for her thistle design. She achieved the outline effect in the quilt by fusing all of the appliqué shapes, not to the background, but to the right side of black fabric. She also applied fusible web to the wrong side of the black fabric to keep the paper intact. The black fabric was then trimmed to within one-sixteenth inch of the appliqué shape, giving it the illusion of an outline. She removed the paper and positioned the double-layered appliqué and permanently fused it. Finally, she used black embroidery floss to finish the stems and add accent lines. "Because Sim Siamdang's insects appear almost comical, I made my insects bold and somewhat cartoon-like."

The quilt borders are not symmetrical. Ruth attached the fuchsia border on the right side as balance to the larger plant on the left. She used fused Ultrasuede for the corner icons. Quilting was kept to a minimum so that the delicate shapes of the plants and insects are the main focus.

Cindy Sisler Simms
Woodbridge, Virginia

36.25" x 44.5"

Cindy teaches quilting and conducts workshops in the southeastern part of the United States. She has made quilts for Shirley MacGregor's other books and was delighted to accept a new challenge inspired by Sim Saimdang's art. "When my plants and bugs design arrived, I planned some color combinations. Then Shirley's packet of Korean fabrics was delivered and I found my planned blue background would not work. I found the right fabric with a subtle touch of glitz in the markdowns at a fabric store while shopping for another project."

Cindy made the flowers using the fuchsia and yellow Korean material. She made the fuchsia flowers with ruching strips and the yellow flowers with stuffed yo-yos. The leaves were created using Joan Shay's method from her book, *Petal Play*. This allows the leaves to have loose edges. To add a spark to the quilt top, Cindy decided to whipstitch around the edge of the leaves with a glitzy thread. "Then the flowers needed to have some sparkle, so I added beads."

Cindy used hand appliqué for flowers and insects, and completed the border cloud designs and remaining work by sewing machine. One cloud design was mirror-imaged to form an "L" overlapping the center background and border fabrics. A satin stitch showcases the pastel colors of the clouds. Two additional cloud designs became quilting designs. Half-circle quilting reflects the fact that dragonflies do not fly straight. Diagonal lines represent the way grasshoppers would jump. Cindy framed the quilt with a black binding to provide balance for the black of the soaring dragonfly.

Chapter 4
Frog

Frog in Silk Pajamas 27.5" x 32"
Shirley MacGregor
Seoul, South Korea

"I wanted to use traditional Korean fabrics and keep to the design. I used 100 percent Korean silk with a distinctive weave for the background. I found the silk difficult to work with, as it slid in every direction. After the basic top was finished, I decided to put a stabilizer on the back so it would stay straight for quilting. I used cotton for the flowers, leaves, frog and insects, and applied the designs using fusible web. The more work I did, the braver I became, using a variety of methods and materials. I made the bee with ribbon and a plastic, fuzzy yarn."

Shirley used a narrow polyester ribbon for the border design. "The problem was, how to attach it to the slippery silk. I taped the top down to my table and marked the placement of the ribbon. I left it taped while I sewed the ribbon down by hand. Then I used a toothpick to apply fabric glue dots to hold the ribbon down. It was a fairly successful strategy, but I am sure there is a better way out there."

A silk backing fabric and an all-cotton batting completed the quilt sandwich, and the quilt was hand and machine-quilted. Shirley outlined all images in silk thread. She quilted the sky using traditional Korean cloud forms, and quilted the border with its ribbon fretwork pattern by hand. The border design is seen all over Korea on walls and buildings.

Shirley MacGregor   Seoul, South Korea

Lily at Dusk 28.5" x 33"
Kris Bishop
Woodbridge, Virginia

"As soon as I saw the design, I pictured tiger lilies in a rich, bright orange, against a purple sky. I was imagining late afternoon. I also wanted a variety of fabrics and textures so I used cotton, cotton lamé, Ultrasuede, beads, silk ribbon embroidery and regular embroidery. I decided to use two fabrics for the background, pieced diagonally."

Kris used the freezer paper method to do her hand-appliqué. She traced the full design onto an overlay of interfacing to serve as a guide for positioning the pieces before basting them to the pieced background. She added dark lavender Ultrasuede clouds to the batik border by first tracing the clouds onto a fusible interfacing. Once satisfied with the placement of the clouds on the border, she ironed them into place.

Kris machine-quilted the veins in the leaves, and used stipple quilting for the sky. One large leaf, a bud and one wing of the small moth, give the feeling of floating free of the background. "I got the effect of what I imagined—a tiger lily, with butterflies fluttering around it, the sun getting lower in the late afternoon sky, the frog in his peaceful place in the tall grass under the leaves as he waits for dark."

Kris, a widow and mother of a grown son, is a retired teacher who has been quilting for over forty years. She enjoys all aspects of quilting, whether traditional or contemporary, by hand or sewing machine.

Bridging Cultures and Centuries   25.27" x 33.5"
Faye Quayle   Pukerua Bay, New Zealand

Faye Quayle

Faye's marriage and her quilting experience have both passed the fifty-year mark. Her quilts have been featured in books and magazines in New Zealand, Japan, and the United States. Faye often teaches quilting classes in New Zealand.

Her quilt is based on a Sim Saimdang work featuring a frog and tiger lily. "A frog! I wondered if Korean frogs are like the New Zealand native frogs, which are about 1" in length. I went looking for frog fabric and found just the right thing. Surprise, surprise—it was made in South Korea! The presence of the frog indicates water and I used turquoise silk for this, with sashiko quilting stitches and beaded highlights." Fabrics sent by Shirley from South Korea show up in the flowers and pink moth. "The Korean silk is slippery, so despite my reluctance to use fusing materials, I have succumbed to stabilizing the silk."

Faye used cotton sateen purchased in California in 1984 for the borders, and applied a tear-away stabilizer to the border fabric for firmness during the machine embroidery. She used a Japanese Hera tool to mark the curved design, and an engineer's radius template for the circles.

"The curved design could almost be a New Zealand Maori one. Similar designs appear in so many cultures. While working on this design I began thinking of possible titles. It crosses so many boundaries of culture, time and techniques. The quilt's title will be *Bridging Cultures and Centuries*."

Chapter 5
Two Pumpkins

Madelaine Hutchin
Sussex, England

Although Madelaine and her husband Charles currently live in Sussex, in the south of England, they have lived in Africa, Asia and the Middle East. Madelaine began quilting over twenty years ago, has studied with the City and Guilds programs in England, and has taught patchwork at a local college. Her work has been displayed in numerous locations throughout the United Kingdom. Eastern fabrics, particularly silks and batiks, are her specialty. She is involved with art and quilt groups in the southern region of the United Kingdom. Charles often helps Madelaine with titles for her quilts.

"I did not want a solid feel to the background of this quilt, but desired movement and a feeling of earthy colors blending. I embarked by first piecing all the colours I saw in my garden to make a fluid base for the appliqué so it would seem as though the pumpkins were growing on an allotment. I have used printed cotton fabrics as the foundation and my treasured Asian silks for the appliqué. The result of this glowing foreground gave me the inspiration for the title of this quilt."

Colour Aglow   32.5" x 46"

A Korean Quilt - Two Pumpkins 41" x 48"

Cathy Sperry   Anaheim Hills, California

Cathy and husband, Dave, have been married for twenty-six years and have two children. With eight corporate relocations over the years, quilting has made connecting with new people very easy. One of her grandmother's scrap quilts on her bed was Cathy's first introduction to quilts. "I remember lying in bed and trying to find the repeat fabrics and studying the design." After earning a B.S. in Home Economics Education at Oregon State University, she taught for eight years in Oregon and Texas.

During one move, Cathy discovered a passion for quiltmaking. "Traditional styles and methods are my preference but I also enjoy pushing myself to try more contemporary designs. I take as many classes as I can and enjoy sharing my quilts through various means such as presentations, teaching, exhibitions, and entering challenges."

Cathy's quilt has a combination of hand and machine work. She used bias bars to make the strips for all the branches and small stems. The majority of the quilt contains cottons and cotton batiks. Some of the Korean fabrics she received as part of the project became flowers, petals, butterflies and a grasshopper. Cathy appliquéd the butterflies and grasshopper to a piece of interfacing she found in one of these fabrics, and hand-appliquéd the insects to the quilt top, adding embroidered details later. The quilt was machine-quilted with a variety of threads, with hand-beading providing the final touches. These beads, blending into the background, provide interest without detracting from the design.

An interesting aspect in the creation of Cathy's quilt is the use of an opaque projector. "The design needed to be enlarged and I prefer to do this myself because I get more of a feeling for the design.

"In planning the quilting design, I realized that I needed the density of the quilting to balance the strong borders and maintain the shape and flatness of the quilt. The 'tumbling blocks' quilting design worked well and helped to make the appliqué design 'pop.' To look like an extension of the border design the binding needed to be the same finished width." Cathy experimented with different widths and found one that worked.

Paul Wank   Eureka Springs, Arkansas

Paul Wank
Eureka Springs, Arkansas

Paul is a retired academic librarian. He became interested in quilting in the late 1980s after many years as a spinner, weaver, dyer, and fiber artist. His involvement in quilting and art quilts has evolved through the creation of fiber art, both on and off the loom.

"I ultimately realized that I could create art by manipulating someone else's fabric—hence art quilts!" Paul derives inspiration from Kathryn Watts, his quilting mentor, and Mary Ruth Smith, a fiber artist from Texas, as well as other quilt artists.

"I like to use the image of cats in my quilts, reminiscent of the Renaissance and Surrealist painters. I am also interested in the use of traditional quilt blocks and quilt designs in the expression of political and social opinions and statements on the current conditions in the world.

"After an Internet search and viewing of Sim Saimdang's work, I came to the conclusion that a literal interpretation of her watercolors would not be possible. I therefore searched my stash of fabrics and quilt shops in the region for fabrics that would express the feeling of the artist's work. I chose various hand-dyed batiks and other cotton fabrics.

"The quilting technique used was the needle-turn method of appliqué, which I felt best expressed the artist's work and my interpretation of it. The choice of the mottled green and white cotton lawn background allows the flowers, vegetables and insects to stand out. This soft cotton fabric was a good choice as a base for the appliqué as it was easy to needle. The leaves, blossoms, melons and butterflies were created from Bali hand-dyed fabrics and a small amount of my own hand-dyed fabrics. The high count of these pima cottons made it easy to appliqué and keep a crease. In fact it made the appliqué part of the quilt a joy!

"The cricket and stems are embroidered. The rest of the quilt top is a commercial cotton fabric of jade green with a washed-out floral print on it. I wanted the effect to be of antique brocade or damask. To enhance this effect I quilted the central portion diagonally using silver metallic thread. The top was designed to look like a traditional Korean painting applied to a scroll. It was quilted in gold thread with traditional Korean designs. My overall goal was to create a wall quilt that gave a sense of looking at an ancient Korean painting that is done in contemporary colors."

Winter Melons   29" x 49"

Chapter 6
Loofa

I Don't Like Butterflies 36.5" x 45.5"

Liz Gray   Eugene, Oregon

"My quilt, *I Don't Like Butterflies*, has a machine-pieced background using the Easy Pieces technique of Margaret J. Miller. I don't like butterflies but knew I had to include them to stay within the original design. I machine-quilted them onto the quilt using a neutral variegated rayon thread and beaded them with clear glass beads. That makes them *there*, but not really." The images on the quilt were created by needle-turn hand appliqué. Silk ribbon embroidery is also featured in the quilt.

Liz is a forty-four-year-old mother of two. She operates a machine-quilting business out of her home and also teaches hand appliqué classes. "I started quilting when I was twenty and pieced my way through the years. Then came appliqué. The love of appliqué has its hold on me. Hand appliqué has given me the vehicle to express my creativity."

Barbara Craig Engler   33.5" x 42.5"

Barbara Craig Engler
Bentonville, Arkansas

"For the Loofa quilt, I knew immediately that I wanted to use a dark background and one in a grayed purple with some texture to it. It is a directional fabric so I carried that line into the border. A contrasting fabric was used for the gourds, narrow frame, binding and backing for continuity. Hand-dyed fabrics from Shades Textiles were used for the butterflies and grasshopper. Several appliqué methods were used in making the leaves, stems and gourds. I truly love appliqué and find each class taken adds something new to my personal style. I prefer handwork and always have a 'carry-around' project ready to take with me at any time.

"Three sizes of pearl cotton thread, some hand-painted threads from the Caron collection, were used for stems, vines and quilting. A little ink stippling helped define the lines in the flowers and butterfly. I hand-quilted around the major shapes and used Linda Potter's *Qwik Stitch* method for the rest of the quilting. Marking quilting lines with the new Clover white water-soluble marking pen solved the problem normally encountered with using a dark fabric. The lines were easy to see and equally easy to remove."

Barbara has lived in Bentonville most of her life. Recently retired, she has taken on more duties in her area's quilt guild. A blended family of six children and six grandchildren keeps her and Bob, her husband of nineteen years, busy. Bob's hobby of making miniature gas engines fosters an appreciation of the detail and time involved in quilt making. He often collaborates with her on quilting projects and has been known to create a gadget or two that makes Barbara's work easier.

Loofah Garden   35.5" x 46.75"

Glenda Beasley   Doha, Qatar

As a military spouse, Glenda has traveled the world, acquiring an impressive collection of fabrics and quilting memories. "Of course the best part about making a quilt is the shopping. I did go a bit overboard with this project." On vacation in the United States, "Land of Many Quilt Shops," Glenda shopped her way across the country looking for the right stuff for her quilt. She found her background fabric in a creamy tan mottled print resembling old watercolor canvas.

Glenda used a variety of greens to make up the leaves, and appliquéd them by hand. She used a freezer paper method to hold the leaf shapes until finally applying them to the background, simplifying the leafy area on the left, and staying true to the design on the right. The grasshopper is appliquéd

broderie perse. "I used a variety of appliqué techniques on this quilt. Along the way I even discovered that I don't hate appliqué."

The loofa fabrics range from green to tan. Glenda's good friend, Andy Bailey, did all of the embroidery while Glenda pieced a dark brown border resembling antique wood. Andy also gave support and advice when it was time to make the flowers. All the major elements are hand-quilted, while the background and border are machine-quilted. Glenda's adventures in completing this quilt make an amusing story (see pg.11). "Without the encouragement and assistance of my many friends and family members along the way, there would have been no quilt. So, thank you one and all!"

Chapter 7
Two Beetles

Christina Brown   Eugene, Oregon
Dragonfly and Two Beetles   28.5" x 42.5"

  Christina has been quilting for three years, and is mostly self-taught. However, she has worked as a graphic designer and artist for the past twenty-five years, and is thus well prepared for this new medium. Although she has retired from her career in design, she is able to apply her knowledge of design and color theory to her various creative projects.

  Finding the background fabric was Christina's most difficult challenge, as she wanted an abstract yet natural look that was light in value to allow the design to come forward. She found a batik that would work, and chose some brightly colored kimono scraps to add sparkle to the foliage, and an iridescent silk douppioni for the border fabric.

  Christina created the dragonfly with free-motion stitching. First, she printed the design on a heavyweight, water-soluble stabilizer. "I lightly glued a sheet of copy paper along the top of the stabilizer to aid its feed through the printer." She then put the design into a hoop and stitched it with monofilament and metallic threads. Then she removed the stabilizer, and beaded the body of the dragonfly.

Christina Brown,
Eugene, Oregon

"I had a couple of problems. I realized I had to work quickly with the air-erasable marker and get my pieces placed before my lines disappeared. When I started to machine-quilt the border design, the gold metallic thread didn't show up strongly enough so I hand-embroidered the design with rayon thread."

After living for many years in Seattle, Christina and her husband have retired in Eugene, Oregon.

Julie Rassmann   Eugene, Oregon   32.5" x 44.5"

Julie Rassmann

Eight years ago, Julie and her husband James moved with their two children from Los Angeles to the Oregon coast. She took early retirement and now enjoys volunteer work, gardening, reading, quilting and other needlework projects. She travels with her husband on business, which allows her time to visit quilt stores across the country. Although Julie has been sewing and stitching for many years, learning to quilt really started with the move to Oregon.

"This quilt combines all the techniques I love. I machine-pieced the background, hand-appliquéd over that and used embroidery stitches for details. I used the appliqué methods in Jane Townswick's book, *Artful Appliqué*. I used silk thread for appliqué on all elements except the scrollwork on the bottom border, where I used cotton thread.

"The design for this quilt came as a surprise. A delicate botanical drawing was emailed to me. Then came the border design and a package of Korean fabrics taken from old traditional costumes. I was challenged and overwhelmed. I decided to use my favorite style of quilting, a pieced background with hand appliqué on top. I also decided to use only fabrics and thread I already owned and those Shirley sent. The beetle and dragonfly wings and parts of the border were made with Korean fabric."

Julie used a variety of threads, floss, yarn and ribbons to add details. "One problem that I encountered was with the "Very Velvet" thread. It moved and stretched after being couched down. The more I handled the quilt while quilting, the more it moved. I ended up with very wavy lines in some places but my friends love the look and thought that I had done it on purpose. This is only my second hand-quilted project."

Two Beetles

Chapter 8
Eggplant

28.5" x 31.5"
So Ra Yoon   Seoul, South Korea

After graduating from Kongwon University in South Korea with a major in fashion design, So Ra has been developing her skills in quiltmaking over the last few years with classes taken in the United States and South Korea. Her first child was born in China during a three-year stay. Now at age 8, Subin is very proud of her mother's work, as is So Ra's husband. So Ra participated in another of Shirley MacGregor's books, when she made a manhole cover quilt based on a design from Hadano City, Japan. That quilt is included in the book, *Treasures Underfoot, Quilting with Manhole Covers, Round 2*. "My mother-in-law was really proud of me after going to that exhibition [of manhole cover quilts] with her friends.

"To be honest, I was more stressed making this quilt. It was made while I was pregnant with my second child and I had morning sickness. The memory of that time is part of the making of the quilt that I will always remember."

So Ra tried to find material that was similar to Han-ji, a special Korean fabric, but she could not. Instead she used a cotton jacquard for the background. This fabric is normally used for sofa or mattress coverings. The foreground fabric has been stitched to give the appearance of rocks.

The purple portions of the eggplants are separate from the background. So Ra used Solvy in the initial sewing process to give a three-dimensional effect to the double-sided vegetables, which are attached at the top stems. She machine-appliquéd the leaves using the fusible web method, and added machine embroidery. "A grasshopper and a gold bug were machine-stitched using Solvy. This is my first experience using Solvy, so it was quite intricate. But the result was better than I expected."

38.25" x 45.25"

Bunnie Jordan
Vienna, Virginia

"I began the sewing process by layering the smaller pieces and sewing them onto lightweight interfacing. This allowed me to appliqué one complete bud section or blossom onto the background so I was not working with many small pieces. A single mottled fabric for the background seemed truer to the simplicity of the painting than a pieced one. I chose several greens for the leaves and used most more than once. Larger leaves were needle-turned for hand appliqué and smaller leaves were fused. Korean fabrics were used for the butterflies and some buds. Fusible bias tape for the branches and border design made later hand appliqué easier. I decided on a water flow pattern for the machine quilting with some outline/echo quilting. The interlacing pattern would be repeated for the border quilting. Embroidery was used for details on the insects and some stems."

Bunnie Jordan works for the National Institutes of Health as a nurse. She has been a quilter since the early 1980s and is a nationally accredited quilt appraiser. Bunnie teaches at the annual Jinny Beyer Hilton Head Seminar and is a Board Member of the American Quilt Study Group, and a member of several national and regional quilt groups.

Instructions

General instructions for turning these designs into quilts are just that—general. We assume that the reader already has a working knowledge of quilt construction and a store of favorite techniques and methods to achieve a finished product. For newer quilters, or those wanting to experiment with the "A" word, we present basic descriptions of appliqué methods.

In the last few years a number of products have become available that make the transition from hand to machine appliqué easier. We have included a list of such products, as well as a few books on the subject, which may help turn your experience into an enjoyable and long-lasting fondness for appliqué.

In the instructions, we suggest an order in which to layer fabric pieces, and each design is numbered for that purpose. If you follow that order, you should be able to complete the appliqué successfully. This is by no means the only way to create a quilt from one of the designs, so if you feel comfortable with your own methods, feel free to jump out of the loop.

Background Fabric

Because some shrinkage may occur, depending on your design and the tightness of your stitching, your background fabric should be larger than the finished size of your project. Once the appliqué is finished and has been pressed (if you desire the flat look), it can be cut to the required finished size.

The background fabric is usually prepared by basting, or *lightly* ironing, the center fold lines horizontally and vertically, and along the two diagonal fold lines. You can center your design within these basting lines either by using a light table, and lightly tracing the design onto the background fabric, or by using a transparent overlay to place the design shapes as you appliqué.

With the transparent overlay method, trace the complete design on the plastic film along with notations for all the fold lines. You then have a reference that can be used during positioning, pinning and basting, and as a final check before appliquéing your design. Once you place the fabric shape in the proper position on the background fabric, it can be basted or pinned to the background fabric, and it is ready to appliqué.

When using film or transparent plastic overlays, draw the entire appliqué design on the film or plastic with a permanent marker. Add notations for the fold and diagonal placement lines using dotted lines. If the design is large, make smaller sections of the design on other overlays. Work on one area of appliqué at a time, checking placement of the pieces against the transparent overlay. Apply the larger film overlay as a final check before moving on to the next section.

Mylar, and the heavier weights of laminating film, are often firm enough to do double duty as template material. Template plastic can also be used as an overlay if your design fits the standard sizes of commercial template plastic. Transparent film, Mylar, and template plastic are available in quilt, art supply and craft stores.

Note: Check your local copy shop, library or school for leftover laminating film. Excess laminating film cannot be reused once it is run through the machine. Offer to recycle it and use it for your transparent overlays.

Hand Appliqué

Hand appliqué at its most basic level involves attaching a fabric shape on top of a larger background fabric. For example, if you want a flower in your quilt with all its curves and small pieces, appliqué can do it for you, one petal at a time. The flower is built by layering and sewing petal units starting with those closest to the background fabric and working up. With practice you will begin to look at an appliqué design and be able to determine which shape should be appliquéd first—the basket or the flower, the leaf or the petal.

Note: Sometimes it is more practical to create the flower as a completed unit by itself and then appliqué it to the background fabric.

For the most traditional method of appliqué, place your template on the right side (meaning the front) of the fabric and trace around it lightly with a fine pencil. If the fabric is dark, use a good quality white, yellow or gray colored pencil with a sharp point. Chalk pencils and wash-out pens are also good for this process. It is best to experiment with any marker you intend to use to be sure that the lines will disappear easily and not return if you iron over them.

Note: Lightly spraying your appliqué fabric with spray starch may help in marking and cutting the shapes as well as in turning under the seam allowance. A sandpaper board is also useful to keep the fabric from sliding when marking.

After marking the appliqué fabric, cut the shape out slightly wider (one-eighth to three-eighths inch) than the desired size, as you will have to turn under a small seam allowance. Once the shape has been pinned, basted or glue-basted to the background fabric, the seam allowance can be gently turned under with your needle or stiletto as you work around the shape.

OPTIONAL METHOD: The entire seam allowance can be basted under before either basting or pinning the shape to the background fabric. In some cases, you can trim away a little of the seam allowance when dealing with tight curves, points, or bulk, but be careful not to cut too close to the fold of the seam.

To hide your stitches when appliquéing, it is a good idea to use thread the same color as your top fabric. This is a general rule but is subject to personal preference. Quilters using neutral-colored silk threads, such as gray, ecru or black, find the thread becomes buried in the fold of the appliqué unit regardless of the color of the fabric to be appliquéd. The use of silk thread means you don't need as wide a color range of cotton threads to match your various fabrics. Using the color of your background fabric instead can give a look similar to reverse appliqué. Using a contrasting color of thread in a blanket stitch, for example, could give a more primitive, folk art look to your work. Experimenting is part of the process.

Reverse Appliqué

Reverse applique is a technique wherein you attach contrasting fabric to the back (or wrong side) of a quilt top, then cut a design in the top to expose the fabric beneath.

Draw your template shape lightly on the background fabric. Cut away the background fabric *inside* the lines of the template to the seam allowance. Apply the contrasting fabric to the underside of the top. Then turn the seam allowance on the background fabric under, and appliqué it down.

This technique is most identified with the molas made by the Kuna Indians of the San Blas Islands. Reverse appliqué creates a depth to designs which can enhance the overall effect.

Freezer Paper Method

In the freezer paper method of appliqué, the slight adhesive quality of the shiny side of freezer paper holds fabric in place during basting and final sewing to the background.

Draw the pattern shape on the dull side of the freezer paper, and cut it out. Attach the paper template to the wrong side of your fabric, shiny side out. Fasten with a pin or basting stitch. Cut around the outside of the fabric template, leaving slightly less than a quarter-inch seam allowance. Carefully press down the seam allowance (only) with a hot iron so that it adheres to the shiny side of the paper. It is best to press around the fabric unit a short segment at a time. Narrow stems and very small units will require more careful pressing. Seam allowances on curves can be clipped at this time to prepare them for turning under. Stray bits of seam allowance or clips on curves can be tucked under the fabric unit as you do the final appliqué stitching. Any section of a seam that will be covered by another unit of the design does not need to be pressed under.

Note: As you are working in a small area with fingers close to the iron tip, a heat-resistant finger covering is useful. The small heating tool used for fusible binding is also an option.

Once you determine the correct position of the fabric unit, press it on to the background fabric. The shiny side of the freezer paper will hold the fabric shape as you appliqué. You may press and baste the whole design at once, or just a portion at a time, whichever you prefer. As with traditional appliqué, you are still working with the concept of layering the design, starting with the unit closest to the background fabric. When the appliqué shape has been stitched down, make a small opening in the background fabric under the finished appliqué unit, and pull the freezer paper out through this opening.

Note: Cutting a larger opening in the background fabric under the appliqué shape is a personal choice. With a larger opening, the batt may fill the space with slightly more loft. This may be a look that enhances your design. You may also decide to add a separate piece of batt to create a look of trapunto, or stuffed work.

Fusible Web Appliqué

Fusible appliqué is similar in some respects to the freezer paper method. Fusible materials have a paper side and an adhesive side, but unlike freezer paper, the adhesive in fusible web is permanent and washable. The textured side of fusible web is the glue side. Attach the glue side to the wrong side of your appliqué fabric by ironing it for a few seconds. It is important not to iron too firmly or too long, or the glue will melt and make the paper hard to remove.

Note: We recommend that you test your fusible web before using it on your project, as such products vary from brand to brand in adhesive strength, from light to ultra-firm. It is best to follow the manufacturer's instructions. Also, use a silicone-based, reusable, pressing sheet when applying any fusible product. It will protect your iron and ironing board cover.

Trace or draw your shape on the paper side of the fusible material. Cut around the design, leaving one-quarter to one-half inch beyond your design. Place your design with the adhesive side of the fusible facing the wrong side of your fabric. Iron it down.

Cut your design out, following the pencil line. Remove the paper and fuse to your background fabric.

Note: Make sure that your design will face the right direction when you look at it from the right side of the fabric. Odd shapes may have to be drawn in mirror-image to get the correct positioning for the shape. To make sure you are getting the design shape and positioning you want, test samples are an excellent idea.

If you have a piece of fabric with a pattern that you would like to cut out and use, place the fusible web on the wrong side of the fabric, covering the area you wish to cut out. Iron it on. Peel the paper off, turn the fabric over, and cut out the design. Then fuse the cut-out to your background. Press with the silicone-based press sheet between the iron and the fabrics. Follow the ironing time recommendations of the maker of your particular fusible web.

Because fusible appliqué does not have a seam allowance it is primarily used in machine appliqué. The appliqué is attached to the background fabric using a straight stitch with a satin stitch over it, or a buttonhole stitch for a primitive look. Other decorative stitches can also be used. Because the top fabrics are completely fused to the background fabric, the background fabric is not cut away under the appliqué.

Some Things to Consider

The quilts that appear in *Quilting in the Morning Calm* are enhanced with a variety of fabrics and embellishments. Along with traditional cottons and silks, the quilters used suede cloth, sheer fabrics, cotton lamé, and cotton batiks.

As part of the project, each quilter received a small assortment of traditional fabrics from South Korea. It was their option to use it or not in their quilts. They used embellishments such as decorative threads, couching, beading, ribbon embroidery and three-dimensional effects. The *suggested reading* list includes books that discuss most of these methods and materials in detail.

Borders

For the "Morning Calm" project, some quilters were assigned a specific border design, while others were offered a selection. The borders could be used as quilting designs or appliqué along the fabric border. Unlike most Western art, an asymmetrical look is a desirable concept in Asian design. Some of the quilters chose to reflect this concept with the use of fabrics or quilting that does not match on all four sides of their quilts.

All of the borders are based on traditional Korean designs seen over the centuries in metal inlay, canvas, wood, stone, ceramics and textiles.

We have provided corners for some of the border designs. However, you do not have to join the corners to have an effective design in your quilt. Also, you can combine one or more borders in the same quilt as appliqué, quilting, or both. You can vary the size and length of a border design by mirror-imaging the design, as in *Arabesque 4-doubled* and *Cloud 3-doubled*, or by linking the design as in *Arabesque 1-connected* and *Arabesque 3-connected*.

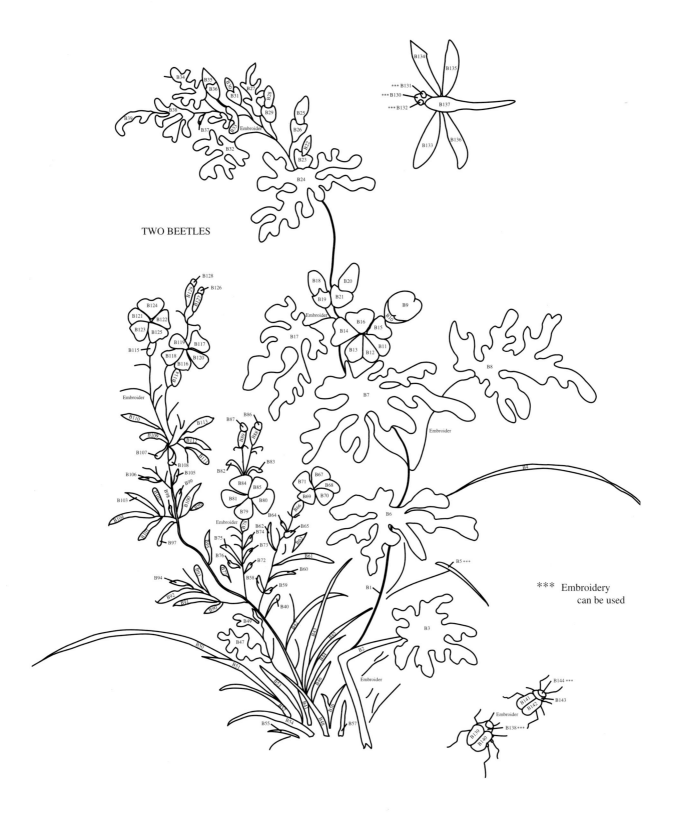

TWO BEETLES

*** Embroidery can be used

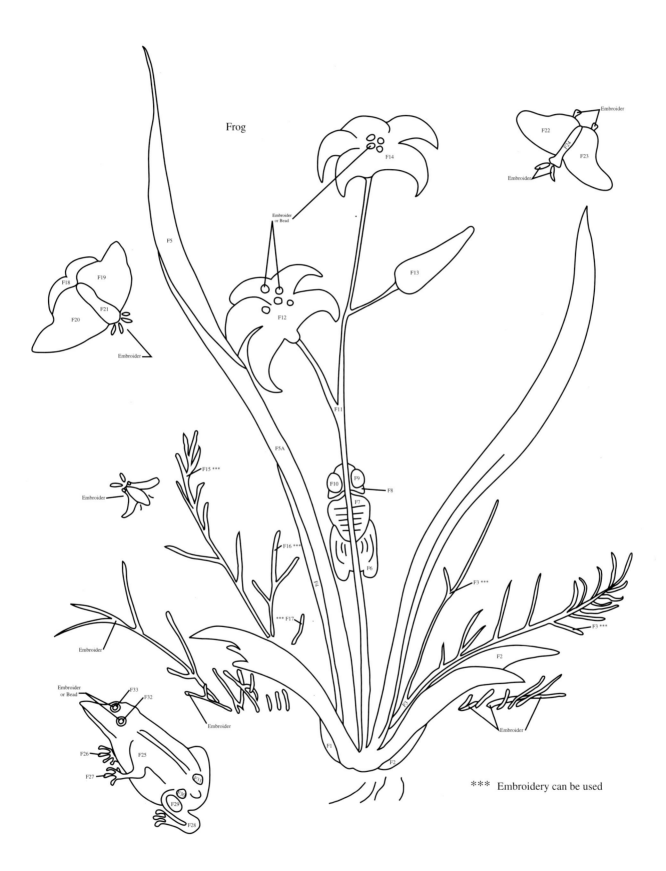

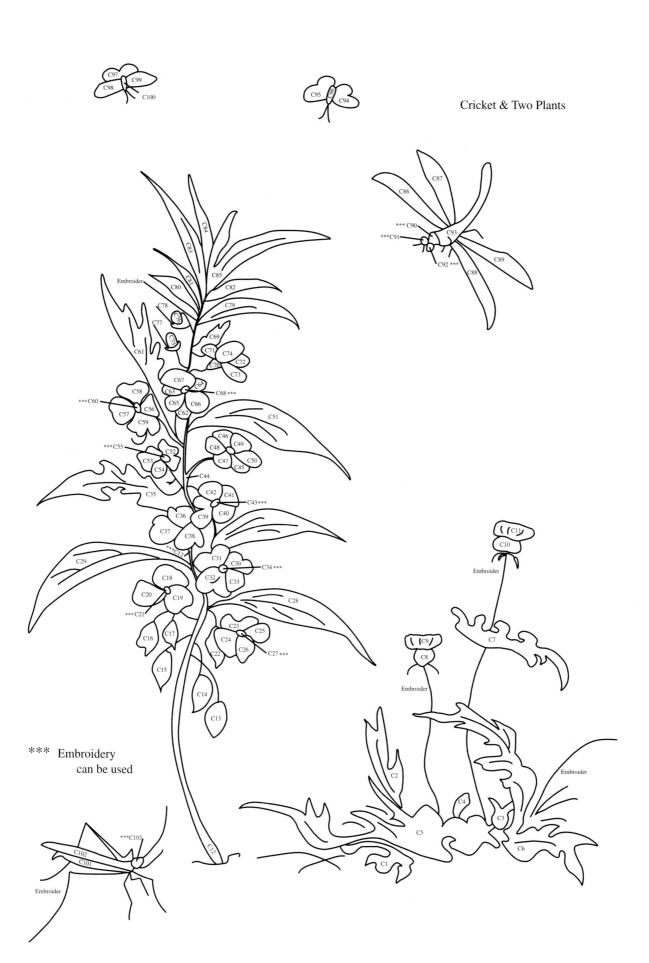

Cricket & Two Plants

*** Embroidery can be used

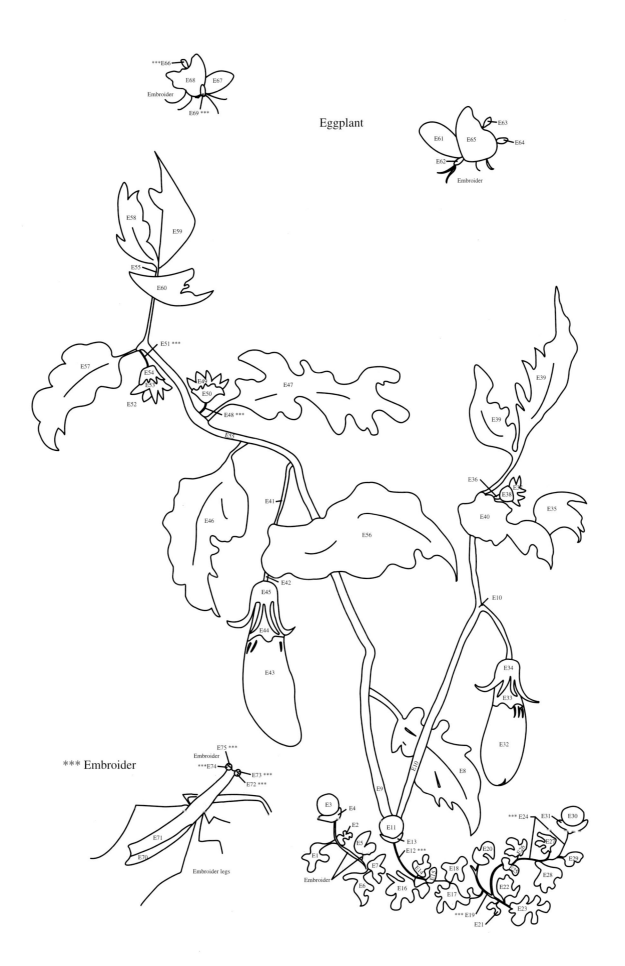

Korean Designs

The border designs found in *Quilting in the Morning Calm* reach far back to the very roots of Oriental culture. Most are of Chinese origin, but have been significant to the art and culture of Korea for most of its long and colorful history.

Many of the themes common in early Eastern design are based on ancient beliefs and philosophies. A number of geometric patterns, such as the *yin* and *yang*, which indicates a balance between opposing concepts, are Taoist symbols. Taoism, in turn, draws heavily from one of China's oldest classics, the *I Ching*, or *Book of Changes*, which describes the use of 64 hexagrams the ancients used to divine the future.[1] The hexagrams, and their component trigrams, are found in various decorative configurations throughout Korea. Four of these trigrams —representing heaven, earth, fire and water— are placed in opposition around the *yin* and *yang* symbol, to form the center of the Korean national flag.

The stylized cloud pattern is well represented in Korean art, and dates to ancient times. Clouds were creatures of heaven, and were at once benevolent, providing life-giving rain to water crops, as well as frightening and destructive, producing lightening, thunder, and torrents of water that could quickly wash away the fruits of one's labor. Clouds also play a role in the myth surrounding the creation of the Korean people.

Other designs entered China, and eventually Korea, through Buddhism, and have been interpreted in various ways by the artisans of the two cultures over many centuries. The Swastika,[2] which unfortunately became the symbol of the Adolph Hitler's Third Reich, has been used in various forms by a number of cultures for thousands of years. In the Orient, it is usually found in a square configuration, with the points facing to the left, opposite to those of the Nazi icon. You will often find it on maps and street signs in Oriental countries as a location marker for Buddhist temples.

[1] The *I Ching* is one of the classic books of ancient China, and the concepts found in it are thought to be more than 10,000 years old. The hexagrams which are central to this work are formed by combining two *trigrams,* each with three lines, either broken or unbroken. The resulting hexagram are used to divine future events, and to guide one's actions.

[2] Swastika (Sanscrit) - is an ancient symbol for good luck or wellbeing.

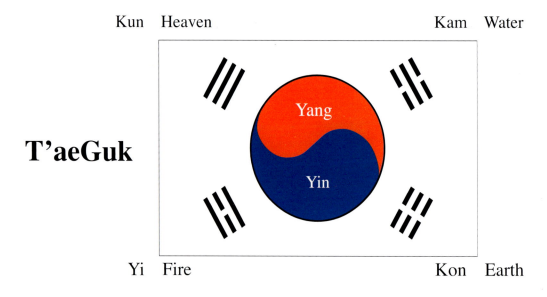

Arabesque 1

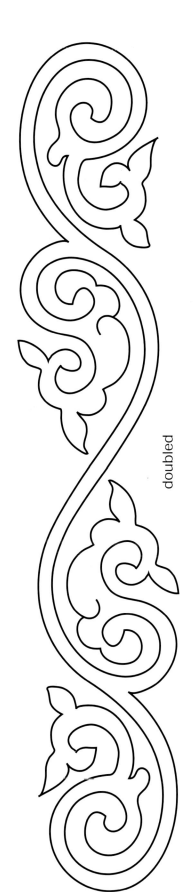

doubled

Arabesque 2

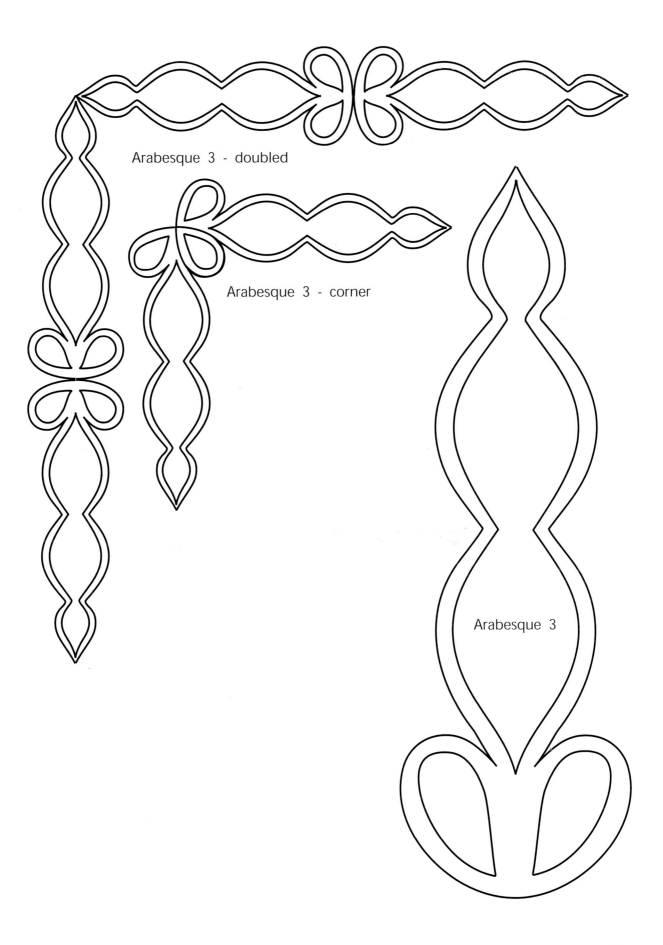

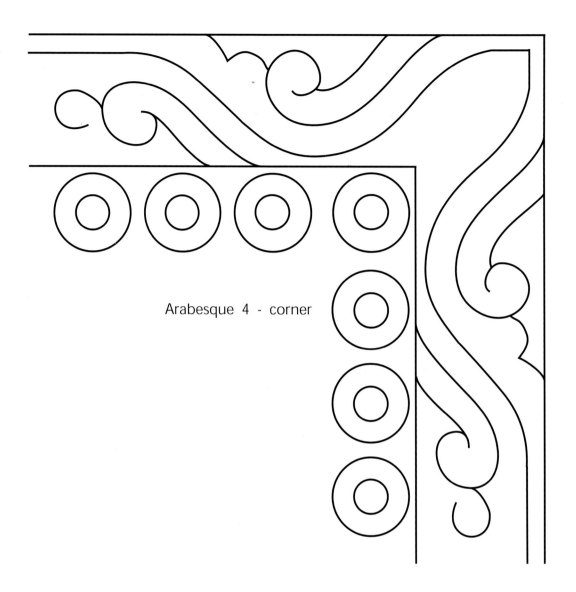

Arabesque 4 - corner

Arabesque 4

Arabesque 4 - doubled corner

Arabesque 4 - doubled

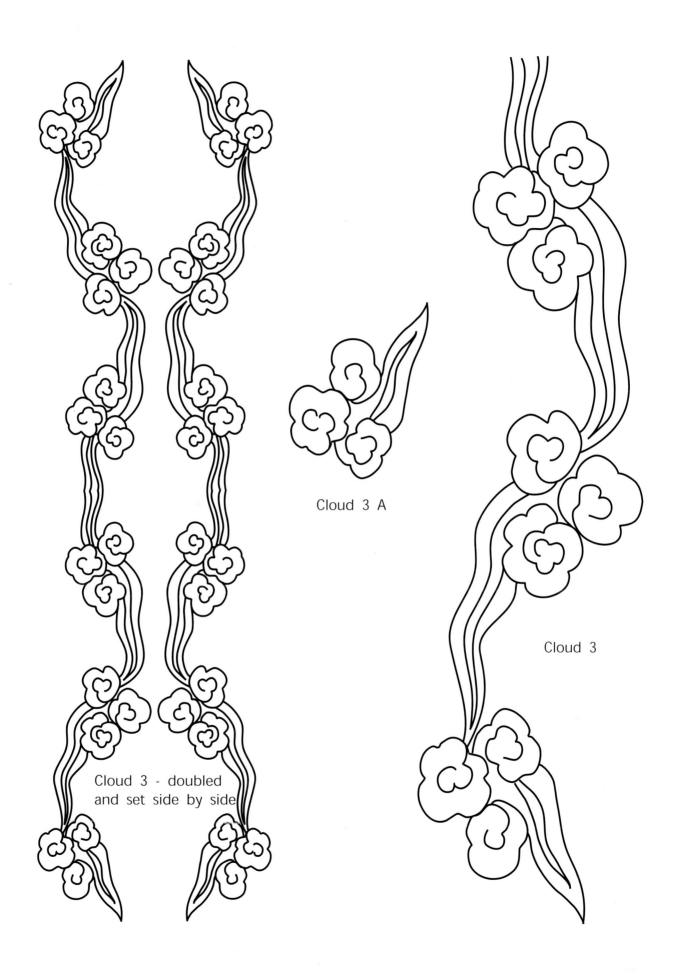

Arch Chain and Crosses

Arch Chain

Crosses

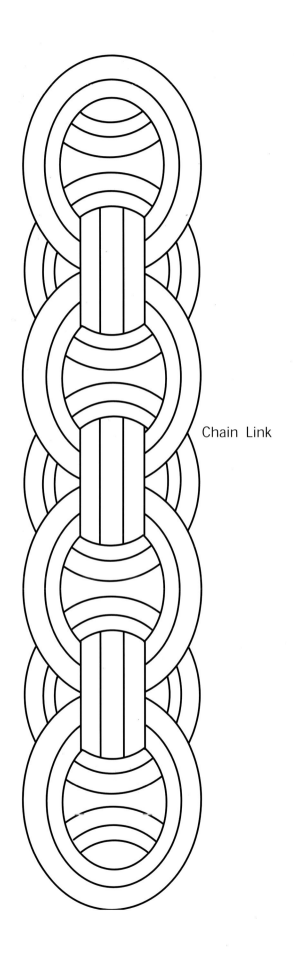

Chain Link

Zig Zag

85

Swastika

Typical design

86

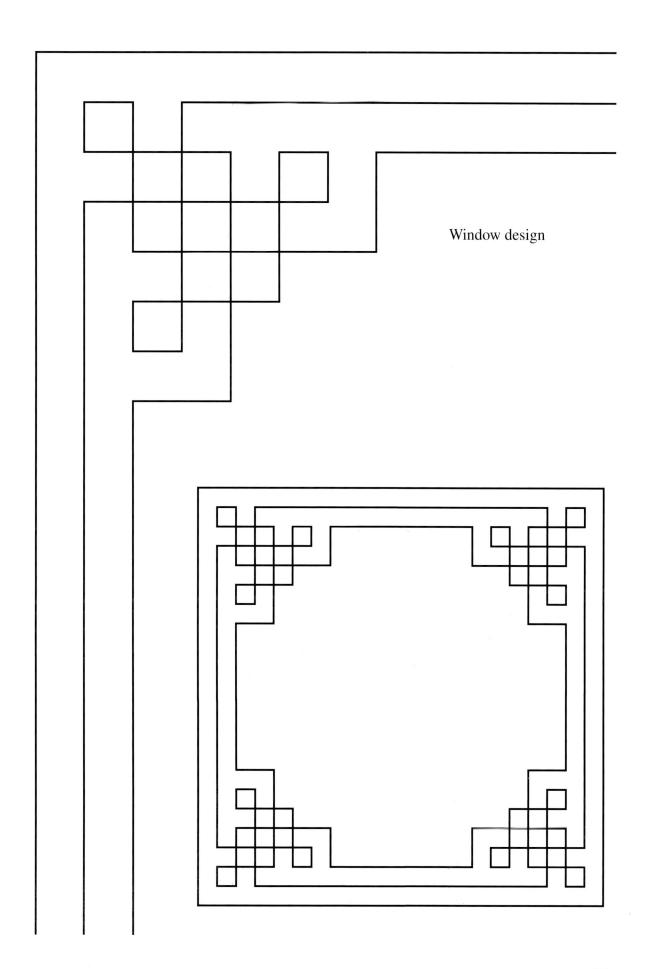

Window design

Border 1   Border 2

Window Quilt Pattern

SUGGESTED SUPPLIES

- Marking

    Mechanical or graphite pencils that draw fine lines.

    Chalk-based pencils such as Quilters' Choice or Clover Marking Pens, for marking on darker fabrics.

- Threads

    Silk Thread: 100 weight in 8 colors: black, white, light blue, dark gray, light and dark natural, light and dark taupe.

    Note: all colors may not be available in your locale but quilting mail-order catalogues or Web sites usually carry a wide range.

    Cotton thread: offers the widest range of colors to match your fabrics. Monofilament thread: in a clear or dark color; it can be used for machine appliqué as well as machine quilting.

- Scissors

    Small scissors with a sharp point are helpful for clipping into tight corners.

- Needles

    Several companies make needles specifically for appliqué. Some quilters use *betweens* quilting needles, others use regular *sharps* needles. Experiment to find which type and length of needle suits your needs.

- Thimbles

    A metal thimble with a non-slip, recessed top is the best.

    There are also products on the market that are metal or clear vinyl pads that are smaller than thimbles and stick to your finger with a temporary adhesive.

- Appliqué pins

    Silk pins 3/4" to 1 3/8" depending on the brand.

    Note: the short appliqué pins currently available are very helpful but easier to lose in the carpet or upholstered chair, so a helpful hint might be to keep a running count of the number you use.

- Finger-pressing tools

    These come in wood or plastic to allow extra pressure in finger-pressing small sections of fabric or appliqué. Handy for traveling or tucking into a sewing kit.

- Ironing

    Appliqué Pressing Sheet: non-stick silicone sheet for protecting your iron when making fusible appliqué. There are several brands on the market in quilt and craft stores.

    Mini Iron

- Adhesion

    Freezer paper: available at supermarkets, with other food-storage products.

    Fusible Web Products: sold under several brand names in pre-cut sheets, as tape, or by the yard in wider widths. Strength of adhesive bond now ranges from temporary hold to very strong permanent bond. We suggest that you experiment to find the type of adhesive best suited to the weights of fabrics you are using.

    Fabric Glue: a water-soluble product specifically for use on fabric. Small dots of the glue can be used for basting to hold appliqué pieces to the background fabric. Make small samples to judge whether this is the right product for your work.

- Light table: handy for tracing design on background fabric.

SUPPLY SOURCES

Keepsake Quilters
Route 25B PO Box 1618
Center Harbor, NH 03226-1618
Phone: 1-800-865-9458   Fax: 1-603-253-8346
Foreign Orders: Please call 1-603-253-8731
Store location: Senter's marketplace in Center Harbor
             (left at first traffic lights in town from west)
www.keepsakequilting.com

Better Homes and Gardens
Quilting
2800 Hoover Road
Stevens Point, WI 54492-0001
Phone: 1-800-709-7000
www.Shopquiltvillage.com

Connecting Threads
PO Box 8940
Vancouver, WA 98668-8940
Phone: 1-800-574-6454   Fax: 1-360-260-8877
Store location: 13118 NE 4th Street
             Vancouver, Washington
              Phone: 1-360-260-8900 x103
www.ConnectingThreads.com

Websites
www.beadstore.com

www.cottonwoodquilts.com/link/hand.htm
       This source provides

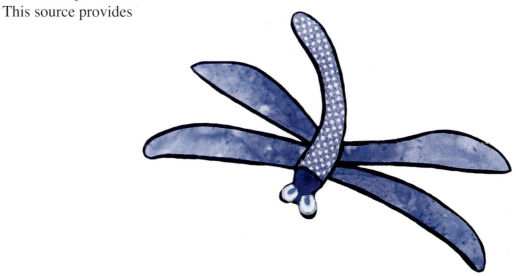

SUGGESTED READING

Color Fusion, Laura Heine, Dragon Threads, 2001. ISBN 0-9641201-5-1
Easy Pieces, Margaret Miller, C & T Publishing, 1998. ISBN 1-571200517
The Nature of Design, Joan Colvin, Fiber Studio Press, 1996. ISBN 1-56477-131-8
The Visual Dance, Joen Wolfrom, C & T Publishing, 1995. ISBN 0-914881-93-0

Blooms and Baskets, Emily G. Senuta, American Quilter's Society, 1998. ISBN 1-57432-716-X
Quilted Sea Tapestries, Ginny Eckley, That Patchwork Place, 1995. ISBN 1-56477-083-4
Snippet Sensations, Cindy Walter, Doheny Publications, Inc., 1996. ISBN 0-945169-20-5

Fantasy Fabrics, Bonnie Lyn McCaffery, Fiber Studio Press, 1999. ISBN 1-566477-272-1
Silk Quilts, Hanne Vibeke De Koning-Stapel, The Quilt Digest Press, 1999. ISBN 0-8442-2081-7

Artful Appliqué: The Easy Way, Jane Townswick, Martingale and Company, 2000. ISBN 1-564772942
Machine Embroidery: Inspirations from Australian Artists, Kristen Dibbs, J.B. Fairfax Press Pty Limited, 1998. ISBN 1-86343-330-9
Mastering Machine Appliqué, 2nd Edition, Harriet Hargrave, C & T Publishing, 2001. ISBN 1-57120-136-X
Petal Play: The Traditional Way, Joan Shay, American Quilter's Society, 2001. ISBN 1-574327704
Thread Magic, Ellen Anne Eddy, Fiber Studio Press, 1997. ISBN 1-56477-189-X
Threadplay, Libby Lehman, That Patchwork Place, 1997. ISBN 1-56477-202-0

The Artful Ribbon, Candace Kling, C & T Publishing, 1996. ISBN 1-57120-020-7
An Encyclopedia of Ribbon Embroidery Flowers, Deanna Hall West, ASN Publishing, 1995. ISBN 0-88195-703-8
The Secrets of Fashioning Ribbon Flowers, Helen Gibb, Krause Publications, 1998. ISBN 0-87341-562-0

Bibliography

Blofeld, John, *I Ching – The Book of Change*, E. P. Dutton & Co., Inc., New York, 1968

Chun, Byung-Ok, *Traditional Artistic Designs in Korea*, Seoul, Po Chin Chai Printing Co., Ltd., 1998

Confucius, *The Wisdom of Confucius*, Peter Pauper Press, New York, 1963

Kim, Sung-Goo et al, *Korean Traditional Patterns: Inlaid Metal Arts – Vol II, Application*, National Museum of Korea, Seoul, 1998

McCune Evelyn B., *The Inner Art: Korean Screens*, Asian Humanities Press, Seoul, 1997

Park, Hyung-Taek et al, *Korean Traditional Patterns: Inlaid Metal Arts – Vol I, Basics*, National Museum of Korea, Seoul, 1998

Saccone, Richard, *Koreans Remember*, Hollym International Corp., Seoul, 1993

Schafer, Edward H., *Ancient China*, Time-Life Books, New York, 1976

Yi, Song-Mi, *Sin Saimdang: The Foremost Woman Painter of the Choson Dynasty*, Oriental Art, Vol. XLVI, No.1 (2000)

Pictures of two sereen paintings courtesy of the Korean National Museum, Seoul, Republic of korea.

Picture of Sim, Saimdang courtesy of the Ojuk'on Museum, Kangnung City

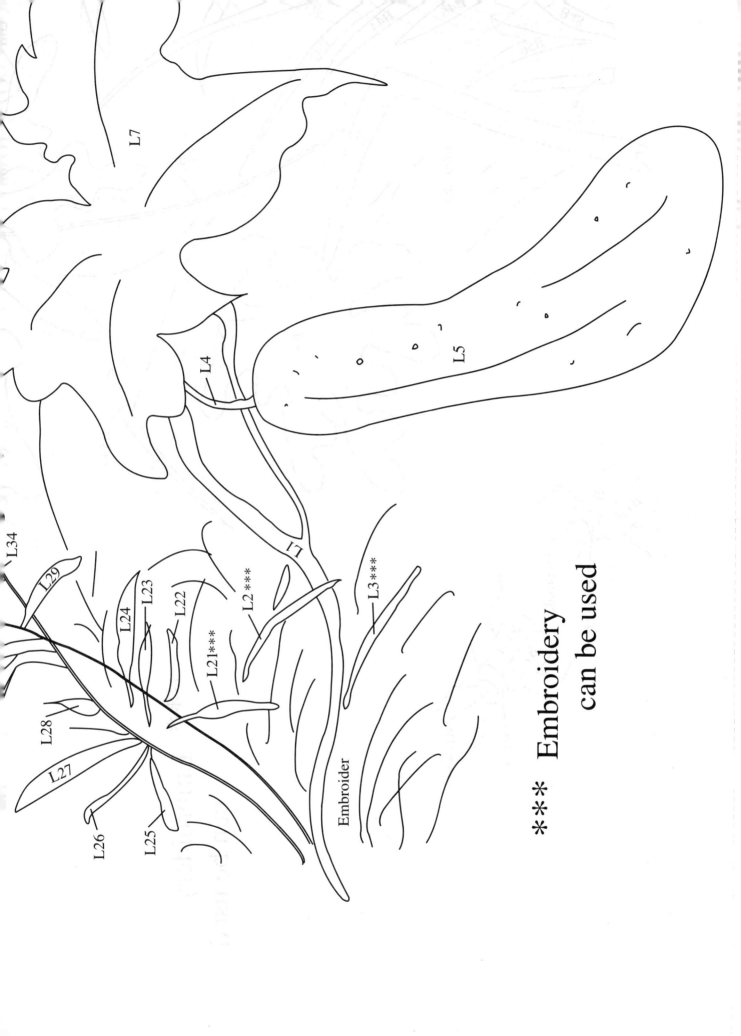

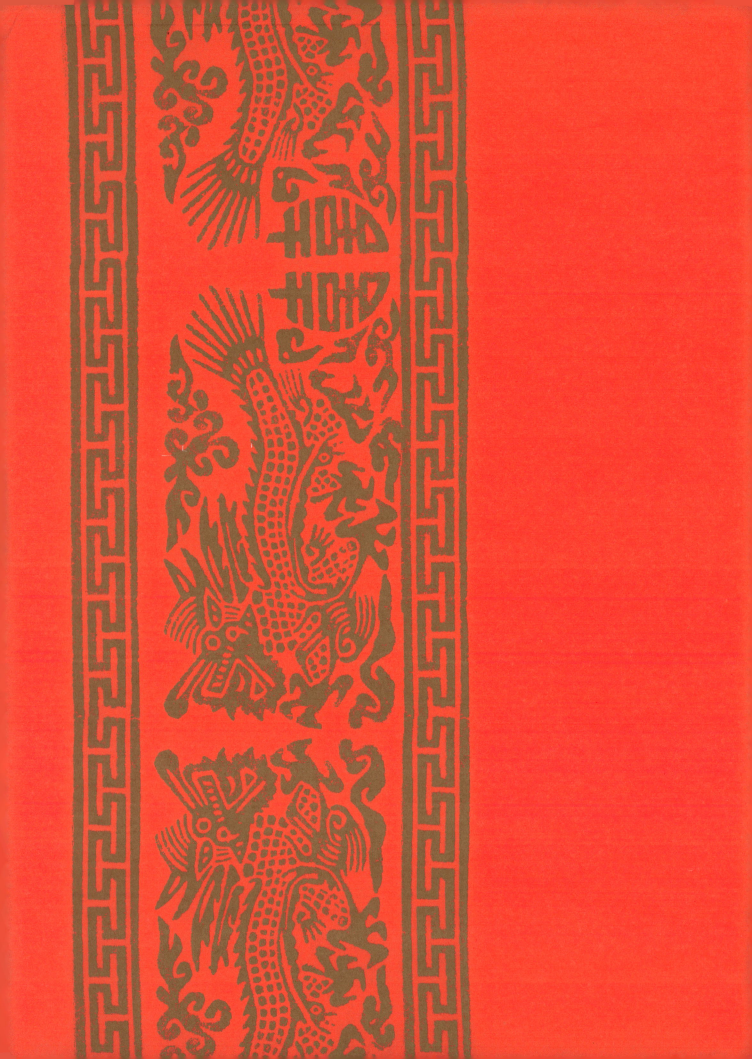

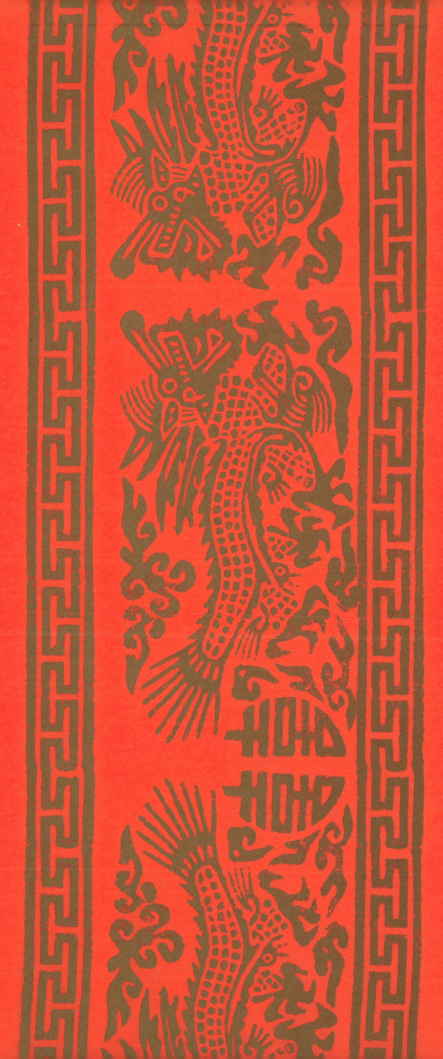